Choose a Better You

Change your mindset – one word at a time

Words by Breed Barrett
Illustrations by Lori Banks

Choose a Better You
Change your mindset – one word at a time

Copyright © Breed Barrett
Illustration copyright © Lor Banks

First Edition 2019
Second Edition 2020

Designed by Fish Biscuit

All rights reserved. No part of this book may be reproduced or transmitted in any form or by any means, electronic, mechanical, photocopying or otherwise without the prior permission of the publisher.

ISBN: 978-0-6484694-6-9

Biography

Breed Barrett, Author

Breed Barrett of Danú is an author, transitions counsellor and tarot reader, having been immersed in giving guidance using tarot and other media for 35 years. Her gift is embodying the qualities of the Goddess Danú, and her spirit guides, to bring a unique Celtic wisdom to you. With Breed, you will receive unique, honest and sensitive insights that will help you on your journey. All sessions include coaching, intuitive reading and guidance to help you navigate your circumstances.

You can contact Breed on danu@danucelticmystery.com, and visit her website at www.danucelticmystery.com

Lori Banks, Illustrator

Lori has always loved drawing and painting. She began her career as a professional artist and illustrator, winning some awards along the way and exhibiting in galleries throughout Melbourne and further afield, both as part of group and solo shows.

Her channelled spiritual work began when she was guided to write poetry and incorporate this into her vibrant energy paintings. Spirit led her to develop and embrace her mediumship skills and spiritual art, and now she creates detailed, visionary pieces imbued with healing energy and colour for clients in Australia and around the world.

You can contact Lori on loribanks@netspace.net.au, or visit her store at https://www.etsy.com/people/loribanksart

Contents

Introduction	1
How to use this book	3
LOVE Let Love in	5
CURIOSITY Keep asking	7
AWARENESS Know yourself	9
SORROW This too shall pass	11
CONTENTMENT Count your blessings	13
INTUITION Trust your inner voice	15
TEARS Let the tears flow	17
JOY Feel the bliss	19
BRAVERY Tear down those walls	21
SPIRIT Immerse yourself in truth	23
PEACE Peace be with you	25
JOURNEY Walk with me	27
GIVE Make a difference!	29
DREAM Believe in your dreams	31
NURTURE Take care of yourself	33
FRIEND Be your own best friend	35
HEAL Forgive yourself and be healed	37
CREATE Create your life	39
BREATHE Breathe easy!	41
SMILE A smile is a wonderful gift	43
ALLOW We all deserve joy	45
LEAVE Don't leave YOU behind!	47
SUPPORT Lean in	49
IMAGINE Imagination is the stepping stone of a new reality	51
WIN/LOSE Sometimes we win and sometimes we lose	53
CHANGE The beautiful butterfly is revealed through the process of change	55
STILLNESS Be still and find your peace	57
VULNERABILITY Open your heart	59
ACCEPTANCE Go with the flow	61
ENDINGS Endings are mere punctuations in life	63
Acknowledgements	64
Help in times of need	66
Endnotes	66

Introduction

What if we could change our inner dialogue by being inspired, one word at a time? What if we could use these words to re-write our story?

What if we feel ready to change, but are looking for the right tools to help us? What if words could heal?

I was inspired by my personal life experience to write this book. It reflects my journey through the pain, suffering and feelings of separation that I experienced in my "dark night of the soul".

What is the dark night of the soul? It can descend upon us as a pervading feeling of sadness, discouragement, or a sense of meaninglessness. My own experience of the dark night occurred through an event that disrupted the status quo, unveiling the reality of my situation.

In my work as a transitions counsellor, I increasingly find that people who come to me for counselling are at some stage of the struggle through **their** dark night of the soul.

Sometimes we move through life in a fairly routine and unconscious way, doing the same things, and probably not doing much self-examination in terms of our life path. The universe has an uncanny way of jolting us out of our complacency! A job loss, a relationship breakdown, the death of someone close, a financial loss — all of these things can catapult us into the middle of a dark night of the soul.

According to Thom F Cavalli PhD, 'if you are searching for your personal alchemy, start with your mess, your crisis, your broken dreams, or your worst nightmares.' This is where we are most vulnerable, and most likely to summon up the courage for a dramatic change.[1]

Stagnation is a killer — we all know that. But complacency is easy! We seem to need a crisis to sit up and take notice of our lives and the direction we are going in. Fear is another great impediment. For instance, it is easier to stay in a relationship than begin the chaos and heartache of leaving.

There is a lot of merit in the suggestion that when we come to a crossroads, take the other road. It sounds simple. Believe me, it is that simple. If you find yourself looking at other options, it may be that it is time to make a change. While it may be daunting, it will be worth it.

> "It is precisely because we resist the darkness in ourselves that we miss the depths of the loveliness, beauty, brilliance, creativity, and joy that lie at our core."
> **Thomas Moore, Dark Nights of the Soul.2**

This book is a tool that you can use every day to bring you back into the light. Think of this book as a companion on your journey as you **envision the life you want**.

How to use this book

The words I have chosen to use are merely psychic vehicles to unlock an emotional response for you and help you change your inner dialogue. They are common words — chosen because of their emotional context — imbued with positive intent for you.

I hope each word will evoke feelings so that you can initiate a positive action, and a change for the better in your life. Ponder on the word and read the accompanying text for inspiration. Relate it to **your** story. How can you apply this positive change today? You can change your story, **one word at a time**. You can nourish your soul and enhance your life.

How can you turn your attitude from negative, depressed, and fearful, to hope, positivity, and to believing anything is possible? Remember, one step in the right direction is one step away from your problems! Every day you wait is another day in the dark. Only you can propel your life forward. It's time to take action for a happier future.

You may have a perfectly balanced and easy life at the moment. Let's face it, we all have different stages in our lives. This book can also help reframe our thinking to keep us from going down the slippery slope of unconscious behaviours and thoughts.

I have produced a guided meditation that you can use every day to create a mindset of positive change. I kept it brief and easy, so you can glide into your chosen word and feel the positive effects. It can be downloaded from my website: https://www.danucelticmystery.com/choose-a-better-you. Of course, the illustrations are also a wonderful focus for your meditation on each word.

Don't be afraid to step out. Everyone in life is on a journey. Everyone has a dark night of the soul at some point; don't be discouraged. This is your moment to make a real difference in your life. Go for it!

Love
Let Love in

"All you need is love", or so the Beatles sang. Yet at times, love can be one of those words that causes us to feel sad and depressed.

It depends on where we are with our loved ones — whether our relationships are positive or negative. It can be that while there is love in them, they don't feel very loving. In spite of what the songs say, love can be hard work!

What is **your** attitude to love? Think about it. Are you open to being vulnerable and letting love in? Or, are you closed off (due to hurt or rejection)?

> Love is the flower you've got to let grow.
> **John Lennon**

Always come from a place of love — even when it hurts. Don't forget, the opposite of love is fear. Fear holds us back from loving and being loved. Use love as the driver propelling you forward, one step at a time, to a new way of being. Think of yourself as a character in a book; you are the one who loves unconditionally. This love makes you strong against hurt and rejection. Make this your story. Look for the light at the end of the tunnel! Look ahead; you'll see that while you might be closed now, you can create a future where you will let love in.

Start by loving yourself. Nurture yourself with positive comments about you. Alter your self-talk. Remove negative and limiting thoughts about yourself. It is as simple as stopping yourself when a negative and self-limiting thought enters your mind. Immediately counter it with positive reinforcement — "I am worthy", I am a good person", "I am lovable".

There are many ways you can help yourself adopt this mindset. Personal development through reading, meditating and self-care should be a priority for you! Every one of us deserves love, but unless we love ourselves, we can be blind to the love other people are offering us.

Let love in! To do this you must be vulnerable and brave; let go of fear. What do you have to lose? Everything that is keeping you from experiencing love!

Curiosity
Keep asking

Be curious about your life — your motives, your feelings and intuition. Life is a big deal. Self-awareness is important. Otherwise, we are unconsciously drifting, and we are not the creators of our own destiny. That is serious! Do you want to be one of those people who arrives at retirement age saying, "Is that all there is?"

> The first and simplest emotion, which we discover in the human mind, is curiosity.
> **Edmund Burke**

Be curious about what motivates you. What do you feel passionate about? There was a time — particularly for post-war babies — when people were compelled to think of their destiny as finding a permanent, pensionable job. It would never have occurred to them to think about what they would **like** to do every day.

Today, this is not the case — not anymore! We now have the luxury of following our dreams. Are you following your dream, your passion? Be curious about what it would take to make this a reality. Consider taking the leap of faith that may help you change direction. Then you can consider the steps that will take you there. For instance, if you want to be a writer, be curious about how writers succeed. Explore what steps will take you from an aspiring writer, to writing every day.

How do you feel about your life? Is it satisfying? Are you content? Being curious about our feelings can help us be mindful of our responses to everything and everyone around us. If you have negative feelings, perhaps it is time to address the trigger — the person, place or thing that triggers these negative feelings. Remember, you are responsible for living the best life you can. It is all in your hands.

Approach every situation with a curious mind. Ask yourself "why?" If this is hard to answer, ask yourself "why not?" There will be an internal knowing about every situation. If you need to change direction, write that "positive way forward" chapter in the story of your life.

Curiosity leads to new places, new thoughts, and new ways of being. It stops the stagnation of playing it safe. It is another way of nourishing yourself.

Awareness
Know yourself

Look around you. Is this the right place for you to be at this time? Is it time you settled, knowing that this is right for you? Should you move on to another place, or another state of mind that you know will serve your life purpose? These are big questions, but the answers are usually simple.

Awareness is empowering
Rita Wilson

Be aware of your friends and family. Do you feel that there is a good balance between supporting them and being supported? Be aware if there is an imbalance. It may be time to reinstate equilibrium in your relationships.

The healthiest relationships exist between those who engage in give-and-take. If there is a toxic relationship in your life — where the other party is all take and no give — it may be time to withdraw.

Self-awareness will help you make the decision that is nourishing and sustaining for you. We can't thrive in relationships that drain us, so practice being able to say "no" to the takers and putting your own needs first.

Be aware of your workplace. Is it supportive of your growth and achievement? Is it a place where you feel valued and can strive be the best you can be? Notice the dynamics between you, your colleagues and management. It is perfectly okay to have healthy boundaries at work and to know when to say no. If the environment is not nourishing for you, it may be time for you to consider your options. In addition, know that you can negotiate better balance in all areas of your life— you just have to speak up.

Many of us exist with the mindset of not belonging. The most important thing to remember is that you need to accept and love yourself, whilst also being aware that we may unconsciously create situations where we feel we don't belong. There are many ways in which we can start the process of feeling included. It begins with stepping out! We may need to reach out in some way to get a sense of belonging. Be aware that when we do nothing, nothing happens. We need to initiate things by taking action. Develop a habit of checking in on your self-awareness so that you can monitor your own wellbeing on a regular basis.

Create your future with this awareness guiding you forward. Without self-awareness, there can be little growth; we are stuck in an illusion of who we are. When we embrace awareness, we can move towards positive change to create a better outlook for ourselves.

Sorrow
This too shall pass

Sorrow is a wonderful teacher. The lessons are hard, but they are worth learning.

Feeling sorrow is the heart's way of telling us that all is not well. It gives us a feeling of regret or loss in some area of our lives. This is a perfectly normal response to life's ups and downs; everyone experiences this at some point. Embrace sadness and grief when life calls for it — don't hold back. No one is immune to this type of emotion.

> One must have sorrow to truly appreciate joy.
> **Megan Hart**

When we experience sorrow and similar emotions, we need to be kind to ourselves. We may experience a range of emotions as we navigate our way through tough times. Know that "all things must pass", so don't resist your feelings. Acknowledging the sorrow and allowing time for it to pass is caring for you.

If you are experiencing sorrow, sit with it; ask yourself what this sorrow is teaching you about yourself. Create a new way of being, knowing that sorrow also brings with it a grace to know yourself a little bit better.

Remember, grieving is not always about losing a loved one. There are other reasons that cause us to grieve, such as losing a friendship, moving house, emigrating, or losing a job. There are many reasons for experiencing sorrow in our lives.

When you are sad, it is a good time to reflect on life's ups and downs, so that you get some perspective. While you may be "drowning in sorrow", it is temporary. "This too shall pass"! Remember the last time you felt sorrow and that since then, you have had something to feel glad about — something comforting, joyful, maybe relieving, something that moved you away from sorrow and into the flow of your life.

This approach can help you to understand that the lesson is valuable and to accept it. You can confidently move forward and realise that as you create your future with a positive mindset, the sorrow slowly loses step with you. Suddenly you will realise you have left it behind.

Contentment

Count your blessings

Are you a "glass half-empty" person? In challenging times, it is easy to think that the world is against you, that you are unlucky and that you don't deserve better. This can be something we are not consciously aware of — perhaps something we have learned from a parent who always had a "lacking" mindset and believed that life is hard. Sure, sometimes it is, but it doesn't have to be.

> I don't look for bliss, just contentment.
> **Alison Krauss**

We all know that there will be times in our lives when we are challenged. The grass is not greener on the other side. Other people's problems are not always apparent, so don't assume they have a perfect life.

Contentment is a wonderful state of knowing what you have, what you don't, and still celebrating your life. It is acceptance of the world's imperfections and the futility of trying to achieve a perfect existence. When we count our blessings twice and our misfortunes once, we are content.

Contentment is a choice. We can choose to be grateful for what we do have — the roof over our heads, food on the table, good friends, rain, sunshine, smiles, laughter, the list goes on! It's those simple things that make us content.

I'd choose contentment over happiness any day of the week! In my experience, we can have brief periods of happiness. Somehow life carries on with its ebb and flow, which makes it difficult for us to maintain these feelings. However, contentment is something we can experience as a state of mind regardless of what is going on around us. We can choose to be content.

When you wake up, practice making your first words of the day those of gratitude. This positive habit will change your point-of-view about the glass being half-empty; you will find yourself enjoying a blissful state of contentment.

Intuition
Trust your inner voice

Do you listen to your intuition? We live in a noisy world with television, radio and our personal devices creating white noise; so much so that we seldom go to a quiet place to tap into our intuition. Our intuition is a powerful tool that helps us know whether what we are doing, or how we are living, is in tune with how our life should be.

> The only real valuable thing is intuition.
> **Einstein**

Your senses guide you every day — touch, sound, sight, taste, smell. Using your sixth sense in small ways every day can help awaken that inner knowing. Start listening to that inner voice. Take the direction it's leading you to.

We just need to find a peaceful place where we can go within and listen to what our intuition is trying to tell us. Think of it as a talent that we have not used for a while. For an example, say you played the piano as a child. You practiced every day after school. So, you could sit at the piano and play several pieces — all because you practiced! It's the same with our intuition, we need to practice every day by tuning in and listening.

Start with a practical exercise. Think about a decision you are going to make. Formulate a question that elicits a yes or no answer. For example, "should I quit my job and change career?" Toss a coin; choose "heads" for yes and "tails" for no. Once the coin gives you your answer, your intuition will give you a big response. You will either know that this is a good decision or a bad one, based on how you react to it. It is that simple! I have yet to try this method without my intuition tapping me on the shoulder in confirmation. Realistically, you don't need the coin —you just have to decide and then sit with the decision. The coin is a tangible thing, helping you to tune in. Do you feel good about it? That feeling is your intuition, helping you to arrive at the right answer.

It helps if you believe you are intuitive. People often comment on other people being intuitive, as if it is a "special" gift bestowed only on a few. That is nonsense! The reason some people seem more intuitive than others is that they practice using their intuition. You can do it too.

There is nothing more empowering than knowing you are in the right place at the right time. So, trust your inner voice to always take you there.

Tears

Let the tears flow

Many instances can move us to tears. We can cry with gratitude, for joy, and of course, we can weep for grief and loss. Tears are such a positive way of expressing our emotions! They signify that our heart is open to all sorts of feelings, and we are dealing with these feelings. Remember this when you try to suppress this very natural response. It is good and healthy. For those who find it hard to shed a tear, I encourage you to let it out and love yourself for doing what comes naturally to you.

> Tears come from the heart and not from the brain.
>
> **Leonardo da Vinci**

There was a period in my life where I found myself unable to cry. It seemed as if I had built a dam around my emotions; I was on the outside of the dam wall and couldn't access my feelings. On reflection, this was a defence mechanism at a time when I couldn't cope with my emotions. I was unwilling to make some necessary changes in my life.

It was some time later — after I had taken a big jump and changed my life for the better — that I realised the dam wall was actually weak. Gradually, it crumbled and I found myself crying at happy movies, at sad movies, crying when I should cry! I was in touch with my feelings again. It was the most joyful feeling.

If you are unable to cry, ask yourself why. It may be that the answer is obvious and that for some reason you are suppressing your emotions because you are unwilling or unable to deal with them. This is a very telling sign and one that you need to acknowledge, embrace and act upon. Your wellbeing is at stake here.

Be kind to yourself, and recognise that your emotional wellbeing is as important as your physical wellbeing. Don't neglect it; cry out loud and weep for joy! Get in touch with the glorious emotions that are there, just waiting to be expressed.

Joy
Feel the bliss

Joy is a magnificent thing to experience. As human beings, we have access to a plethora of ways to experience joy. Bliss, ecstasy, elation, rapture — we can experience all of these without the need for any substances. Meditate on a sunrise, listen to a song you love, revel in the birth of a baby and enjoy the unconditional love of a child. Live with the outlook that there are many ways and reasons to experience joy.

> Joy is the simplest form of gratitude.
> Karl Barth

Let joy in! Know that you deserve it. In my experience, there are a couple of significant factors that contribute to **not** feeling joyful. One of them is fear. Are you afraid if you experience joy, it will be taken away from you? Are you worried that by being joyful, you will make yourself more vulnerable? It is okay to be vulnerable sometimes. Just trust the flow and the river of emotions that are part and parcel of life. Sure, there will be times when you don't feel joyful, and that's okay, but don't make this your focus. That is often an unconscious way we keep ourselves from feeling content.

Another reason we deprive ourselves from feeling joyful is guilt. We think that for some reason (usually completely irrational) we don't deserve to feel joyful. Perhaps we were goaded into feeling guilty by manipulative parents or an unsupportive partner. Maybe we have made it our habit to feel unworthy because other people treated us as if we didn't deserve the good things in life.

This is a perfect time to allow yourself that which every human being deserves. Today, make a conscious decision to discover what makes you feel joyful. It may be a good day to go for a walk, enjoy nature and listen to the birds singing. Watch the dogs playing in the park and the children enjoying the playground delights. Life can be grand if we stop and smell the roses.

Bravery
Tear down those walls

Bravery is a powerful word. When we think of bravery, we think of our war veterans, the police and emergency services personnel. We do not realise it can apply to us. Yet, every day when we make the decision to get up and face whatever the day brings, it is an act of bravery. This is especially true for those of us who are chronically fearful, due to our upbringing or circumstances that damaged our sense of feeling safe in the world.

> Bravery is the engine of change.
> Aisha Tyler

When we think of the word present, we see that it indeed is a gift. If we look at the past, we realise that it is gone and not coming back. Conversely, if we look to the future, it is not here yet, it is not now. But we always have the present moment! If you want to change your life from living in fear, just remember that at this moment there is nothing to fear. You can't worry about what has been and what is coming will not change if you do so. So, revel in the now.

Convince yourself that right now is a great time to be brave. Apply for that job you don't feel worthy of getting. Reach out to someone you would like to connect with. Walk away from that job, environment or relationship that is not good for you. There is no time like the present to be brave.

This is the magic of releasing fear — the biggest stumbling block on our journey. You may think that this is easier said than done. You are right, especially if you have been living with fear as your default state all your life. It is a challenging habit to change but it's certainly not impossible.

Think about where fear may be holding you back from being the best version of yourself. Bravery in times like this is just a decision — a liberating one. It may be that you need to make this decision every day, over and over again. They say practice makes perfect. If you free yourself from fear, you will realise all the possibilities that are open to you — you are invincible.

Take baby steps and gently bring that metaphorical wall down, brick by brick. You will surprise yourself.

Spirit

Immerse yourself in truth

Being spiritual is all about living your truth, seeing the truth in others and not compromising your truth for anyone. In the words of French Philosopher, Pierre Teilhard de Chardin, "We are not human beings having a spiritual experience. We are spiritual beings having a human experience." Looking at yourself this way simplifies your feelings as a spiritual being. This has nothing to do with religious beliefs. It is more about honouring yourself and being authentic.

> A strong spirit transcends rules.
> **Prince**

It is easy to be swayed by the many distractions of life. One way you can continue being the best you can be, is to immerse yourself in truth. Try not to make excuses for yourself; hold yourself accountable. The other side of this coin is allowing yourself to make mistakes and rectifying them where possible. This is not to say you should make excuses and let yourself off the hook. It's about self-awareness, remedial action, forgiving yourself and moving on.

Our spiritual side enriches our lives when we honour it. When we acknowledge the mysterious connection we have with nature, animals, our planet and the whole universe, we are the richer for it.

Being authentic is the most spiritual way to live. By never compromising on who you are and how you are, by never making excuses and putting yourself down, you are honouring your spirit. By nourishing yourself, body and soul, you will give yourself every opportunity to thrive.

Again, take time to immerse yourself in nature. Sit and observe the moon and the stars. Feel the immensity of the universe we live in. Knowing that each person is an integral part of it, you will understand the power of your spirit. Our spirit is what motivates us to connect with others, to go deep within and to commune with nature.

Don't feel you have to be perfect! Just be authentic. We are all human. So, be as forgiving to yourself as you are to others. Let that spirit shine.

Peace

Peace be with you

Peace is a word that evokes images of tranquillity, serenity and freedom from anxiety. One of the greatest gifts we can give ourselves is peace of mind. How do we achieve this?

First, we need to take a long, hard look at our levels of anxiety and worry. Anxiety and worry can become bad bedfellows; feelings we wake up with and accept as the norm, every day of our lives. This does not need to be the case.

Doing a self-audit for a week or so is helpful. Make it your objective to observe the mental state into which you awaken. Do you automatically turn on anxiety and worry? Do you, for a brief moment, feel gratitude for waking in the world yet another day? This "brief moment" is our natural state. Grasp it and tell yourself that this is how you are going to feel. Make the decision that you will no longer give "airspace" to anxiety and worry.

Of course, there are going to be times when we are anxious, when we worry about something or someone. It would be almost impossible to alleviate that from our lives. However, when you think of the word peace, think of how it makes you feel. The word can be a meditation in itself; you can feel a sense of calm come over you when you ponder on the word.

> All we are saying is give peace a chance.
> **John Lennon**

The more people in the human race that embrace a sense of peace, the more it will spread worldwide. You may think that you (just one person) cannot make a difference, but you can — not only to yourself, but also for the greater good.

Journey
Walk with me

Life can be seen as a journey with rites of passage through all its stages, from infanthood to old age. If we view life in this way, it is easy to pinpoint where we are in our own timeline. We can examine where we are at, how we feel about our progress, and look to the future with resolve to fulfil all our aspirations along the way. For why else are we here? We don't have to be philosophical to plan our journey and whilst we map it out, we need to be flexible enough to realise that it is okay if those plans change.

If we don't view our life as a journey, we can become stuck. We can find ourselves ensconced in the here and now. Alternatively, we can become caught up in looking back with regret instead of looking forward with hope and optimism.

Where are you in your journey right now? Are you feeling stuck? That feeling is an illusion, even if you are in circumstances where you think there is no escape. Take a step back and visualise your hypothetical timeline, from start to finish. Imagine there is a dot on the line where you see yourself at present and see that whatever's holding you back is temporary.

Believing that you have the ability to move forward will shake the permanency of this feeling. Keep looking forward – planning, visualising, and hoping for the next phase of your life. Enjoy this process; anchor it in the here and now.

> Every day is a journey, and the journey itself is home.
> **Matsuo Basho**

This journey is **our life.** So, no matter where we are on our path, it is the right place for us at this time. What is important to remember is that if we make a mistake, it doesn't mean we are on the wrong train or at the wrong airport; we have a slight delay in plans. There is always another train, a bus to a different airport, and the opportunity to get back on track.

Be kind to yourself on this journey that's full of wonder, even if it does not always feel wonderful.

Give
Make a difference

When we are born, we are totally dependent on our parents/guardians to sustain us. We spend our days and nights receiving — love, attention, nourishment. Eventually, we start giving back with a smile or a gurgle in response to the loving care we receive.

Again, when we are dying we are totally dependent on our carers to sustain us. The way we give back is by allowing them to care for us. Their giving is to us by means of care; our giving to them is by means of acceptance.

In-between these two stages, we must learn to engage in a lot of give-and-take if we are to survive and thrive in this world. It is a two-way street, this giving! We must give to those who need, selflessly and with love. Yet, we must receive from those who wish to give to us, so that they can know the joy of giving.

> For it is in giving that we receive.
> **Francis of Assisi**

Are you a giver? Do you share your life, your wealth, your table, and your thoughts where you can? There are many ways to give. Sometimes we feel we have been "taken from" and begin to close the door on giving. We decide that the world is a selfish place, and that no one appreciates our generosity. This thinking not only hurts others, but it hurts us too!

If we were to take a step back and look at the best moments in our lives, we'd see they involved either giving, receiving, or both. This is not just about material things; it is also about giving time to someone lonely, giving your attention to someone who feels neglected and unloved or giving love to someone who needs it.

You may believe you have nothing to give — think again. Each and every one of us can make a difference, even if it is giving a smile to a stranger or lending a helping hand to someone in need. To nourish your soul, there needs to be giving and receiving. The whole world flourishes when we practice generosity in thought, word and deed.

Dream
Believe in your dreams

As a child, we live our dreams. They are quite vivid, and sometimes we don't differentiate between dreaming and reality.

As we mature and that old chestnut that is reality sets in, we seem to allow our dreams to dim as we focus more on our responsibilities. The here and now takes precedence over our hopes and dreams. Yet, it is a sad life — one without dreams!

Dreams are vehicles for hope and optimism. We can dream (whether awake or asleep) about a future where we are happier, more content, more fulfilled, more successful — the list goes on! Without allowing ourselves to dream, we are giving drudgery and pessimism permission to be in the front seat.

> Dream as if you'll live forever. Live as if you'll die today.
> **James Dean**

Consider, for a moment, your personal dreams and aspirations. Are you optimistic about realising your dreams? Do your aspirations enable you to strive for a more fulfilling life? Dream is a mighty word. Give yourself permission to think about your wildest dream and visualise yourself achieving it. It's in your hands. Remember, the only thing between you and achievement is the steps you put in place to get there. It is that simple. You want to write a screenplay, to be Prime Minister or an astronaut? Why not go for it?

For all of these possibilities, it is simply about knowing what is needed and creating a plan. Before you say, "well that's alright for others, but not for me," there are many inspirational stories about people who went from "rags to riches" against all odds. Don't be your own worst enemy by making excuses for yourself. First, have a dream, then make it a reality — it's the ultimate way to live. You may find that what you once thought was a dream is actually just the direction you take towards your ultimate fulfilment.

Nurture
Take care of yourself

The word nurture conjures up images of mother and child, and of the physical care that a baby needs.

There are many ways to nurture yourself — through healthy food, exercise, education, the arts, not to mention friendship and love. To nurture yourself as a human being is to live life to the fullest. Another important aspect of ourselves that needs tending is our spiritual being. On this noisy, busy planet, it is one we can get distracted and forget to nurture.

> Nurture your soul.
> **Avina Celeste**

Think about how well you nurture your spirit. Do you live entirely according to the clock? Are your days determined by getting up, working, and going to bed? Make time in your life to nurture that part of you that cannot be satisfied with just the material world.

Our connection with nature can foster that inner joy, that feeling of connection that no pay cheque will give us. Make a habit of watching the sunrise. Marvel at the birds that fly so high above. Observe the river as its currents rush towards the ocean. Spend time with your pet, experiencing the joy of living through his or her eyes. Walk barefoot on the beach and let yourself dance in the rain. The simple pleasure of enjoying nature will nurture your spirit, your soul.

Meditation is another powerful tool to connect with and nourish our spirit. It is a time spent focusing on our inner being, letting go of worldly cares and distractions and connecting with spirit. A daily practice does not have to be onerous; you can start by meditating for 5-10 minutes. As you progress, you can increase the time you spend on this inner journey, for as long as is comfortable for you.

You can light a candle as you set your intentions — an offer of prayer for a loved one, a request for a resolution to a problem. Focus on the flame; it can be quite hypnotic and can draw you into a meditative space where you can send positive thoughts out to the universe, and back to you. Nurturing yourself is one of your primary responsibilities. Remember, if you don't nurture yourself, it is impossible to continue nurturing others.

Friend
Be your own best friend

Looking at social media today, the hype about friendship is rife. You can count how many people "friended" you online. You can feel like a voyeur reading all the information that your so-called friends share publicly. Is that true friendship? Does it fulfil you in a way that a real friend does? I don't think so.

Having a true friend is like finding treasure. You can share your problems, your joys and concerns with them. You can celebrate with them and commiserate with them. Whether you laugh, cry, shout or whinge, they are there for you through thick and thin.

Some friends come and go. There is a saying: "People come into your life for a reason, a season or a lifetime" (author unknown). This is true! We befriend people in all sorts of scenarios. It is the lifetime friends that sustain us long into our old age. They are there with us for the highs and lows and do not judge us.

> A friend is what the heart needs all the time.
> **Henry Van Dyke**

There is another kind of friendship that is important too — the friendship you have with yourself. If we have a problem liking ourselves, our relationship with others is fraught with risk. How do you even believe other people like you, let alone love you, if you don't like yourself?

Remember you are a unique individual and accept yourself exactly the way you are. No one is flawless, even if they think they are! But we are all perfect in our imperfection; this is what makes us unique.

How do you become your own friend? Why not practice in front of the mirror? Look at yourself. Make eye contact. Gaze upon yourself with compassion and love. Think about one of your good friends and how that person feels about you. See? You do deserve to find a friend in you. When you gaze at yourself, don't just pinpoint the flaws and imperfections.

Look into the eyes of your reflection and declare your friendship. Tell yourself that you will put your trust in yourself and always be honest and true to you. Now, think of something funny — laugh with yourself! Watch the reflection as your eyes crinkle with laughter. See? You are fun to be around! You are worthy of friendship. It must start with you.

Heal

Forgive yourself and be healed

We all need some healing. We are all broken in one way or another. We are here on this earth to learn about healing and about improving our attitude towards our beautiful planet. This is the big picture. On a smaller scale, each one of us reflect the broken planet in some way. We hurt each other, we hurt ourselves, and we forget to have respect.

So, how do we begin the healing process? Forgiveness is a great place to start. If we can focus on forgiving others for their transgressions and the perceived hurts they may have caused over time, and if we can forgive ourselves for the times we hurt ourselves and others, we are on a healing path.

Everything we do in the name of healing restores us. We can make decisions about products and services that harm our planet, so that we are not participating in the damage they cause.

> For me, the healing process starts with graciousness and forgiveness.
> **India Arie**

The word heal may be small, but it has an enormous impact, both personally and globally. Think about where you personally could benefit from healing. Are you taking care of yourself physically, spiritually and mentally? Are you respecting your needs? Ponder on what it would feel like to be healed — to feel whole again. What would this mean for you? Living with integrity is profoundly transformative. When you prioritise your personal integrity and health, you can inspire others to do the same. Not only that, you can help others heal when you have done so yourself.

By caring about your own wellbeing, the wellbeing of others and of the planet, you will find yourself making decisions that have a positive impact on your life and the lives of those around you. You do not have to be an eco-warrior to make a difference! What I mean is, you don't have to be spearheading protests, sailing on ships or writing poems of protest. All you have do is be a shining example of living authentically with healing in mind.

Think about three small things you can do to help yourself heal. Once you have mastered these, think of three small things you can do to help heal your community. And on it goes, until what you are doing is making a significant impact. We are all healers — we just need to heal first!

Create

Create your life

What if I told you that you are a very creative person? Around 30% of you will agree; the other 70% will probably say: "No. Not me!"

We are all creative! Maybe some of us misunderstand the meaning of the word. This is no surprise, as we have many businesses calling themselves "Creatives". This infers the rest of us must be totally reliant on them to produce something creative for us. Yes, these business **are** creative. The difference between them and us is that they know they are!

> Write it. Shoot it. Publish it. Crochet it. Sauté it, whatever. MAKE.
> **Joss Whedon**

There are many ways to create. Creation is a process through which we grow and develop. We create opportunities for ourselves to participate in life. We create friendships by reaching out to other people. Bonds are created through nurturing and caring for our children, the elderly and the community.

Accept yourself as a creator. It will give you confidence to know that you are the author of your own destiny. This is not about taking control and never letting go, it is about creating an environment and having a mindset conducive to you moving towards a future you wish to make manifest. There are no guarantees of a fairy-tale ending or that there won't be disruptions and disappointments along the way, but without the vision to create a future for ourselves, we remain stuck. No one else is able to do this for you.

The other side to creation involves using your talents. People create music, artwork, meals and clothing — the list is endless. Acknowledge your unique talents and skills! Practise makes perfect, so keep focusing on the process. The creative process is both practical and spiritual — indefinably satisfying! Practise is hard work; the process can be long, but the results are worth it.

Breathe

Breathe easy!

Breathing is easy — right? Well, if we observe our breathing for a day, we will realise that it changes depending on what we are experiencing. It can even become a habit not to breathe deeply enough.

Ask someone with asthma about breathing. It is something we take for granted, but one asthma attack will leave you treasuring every moment that you breathe easy.

"Breathe easy" —another way of saying there is nothing to worry about. So, breathing is intrinsically connected with how we are feeling. Those who meditate or practice mindfulness become conscious of their breathing and practice control. Controlling our breathing can give us very positive results. Think about when you are at work, having a stressful day. How is your breathing? Is it shallow and fast, or slow and deep? If it is rapid, you can deliberately slow it down and take deeper breaths.

> Breathe. Let go. And remind yourself that this very moment is the only one you know you have for sure.
> **Oprah Winfrey**

Breathe to help combat negative emotions. When you are upset, stressed, worried or anxious, become conscious of your breath. The very act of doing this separates your consciousness from whatever overwhelming emotion you were experiencing — even if for a few moments. That is a good thing. Any time you spend removed from negative feelings is good for your body; your breathing is a wonderful tool to take you away from these feelings.

If you don't believe you can meditate, practice controlling your breath — you are half way there. In my experience, a busy mind finds it hard to meditate. For this reason, guided meditations are good, as they give us something to focus on. Breathing keeps us alive. It can also keep us calm and increase our sense of wellbeing.

To breathe is something we take for granted. Yet if we change our thinking from breathing being something we unconsciously do to something we can consciously focus on, it will improve our lives.

Smile

A smile is a wonderful gift

All it takes is a smile — to brighten someone's day, to make a child feel happier, to break the tension when things are strained.

> Peace begins with a smile.
> **Mother Teresa**

Never underestimate the transformational power of a smile! Granted, there are times when smiling is the last thing that we feel like doing. In fact, we can easily make it a habit to never smile! When we go through a difficult time, and we are always in a state of angst, our facial responses will probably reflect what we are feeling. Our neural pathways will memorise this; our default facial expression can become serious, even stern.

However, all is not lost. You can practice smiling! Every day stand in front of your mirror and smile to yourself. Look at your eyes. Are they smiling too? Make sure all your facial muscles are engaged in the smile. You will find that you start feeling better immediately.

How do you feel when a stranger smiles at you? It is a lovely thing — that stranger's smile. What a gift when you are feeling sad or lonely. Make a habit of smiling at your family, your friends, and even at people you don't know. The world is a better place when you smile. You have the power to lift someone's spirits with this simple action.

Tears of Joy – the number 1 emoji

According to "The Verge" website, Emoji Tracker (which monitors in real time emoji usage across Twitter) has the humble "face with tears of joy" emoji at the No. 1 position across the entire social media site — by a fairly massive margin.

People respond emotionally to smiles, even when they are feeling sad, so never underestimate your ability to help someone with your infectious smile.

Allow
We all deserve joy

Do you allow yourself to dream? Do you give yourself permission to live your life to the fullest? If you don't, why not?

Some of us are suppressed by belief systems embedded in our psyches through controlling parents or an overly religious upbringing. We then seem to go on with our lives allowing these ideologies to make us feel unworthy. We start to think it is inappropriate to put our own desires first.

Believe me, it isn't! As long as you take responsibility for your wellbeing, your role in your family and your job, the rest is up to you. No one has the right to tell you how to dream and what to wish for. No one should be allowed to make you feel unworthy.

> If your world doesn't allow you to dream, move to one where you can.
> **Billy Idol**

The choice is yours. Allow yourself to determine what you would like to achieve in your life and go for it. Read about people who, against all odds, achieved great things. As I mentioned before, there are so many inspiring stories out there. Many, many people have lived lives beyond their wildest dreams.

It only takes determination to change your thinking. Mull over what you won't allow yourself to do, think or believe. Does it involve your career, a creative pursuit, a relationship? What do you need to put in place to start allowing this into your life? What obstacles need to be removed so that you can move in the direction of making your dreams come true? Wishing is good. But the action is needed to get you to a place where you feel comfortable allowing yourself to receive the life you wish to live.

> The harder you work, the luckier you get.
> **Gary Player**

It may seem from the outside that some people are lucky. Generally speaking, the lucky people are those who focus on their dreams and believe they can achieve them. Not only that, they give themselves permission to be successful. Some of the obstacles are within us. We need to make sure that self-sabotage is not at play, that somewhere deep down we don't feel we deserve what we want. Everyone deserves to be happy. Allowing yourself to believe this is important.

Leave
Don't leave 'You' behind!

Leaving sounds like such a final thing to do. Whether it is a town, a country or a relationship, it sounds irrevocable.

It can be, but it doesn't have to be. Leaving can be an important part of your life journey.

> Now, bring me that horizon.
>
> **Johnny Depp, as Captain Jack Sparrow**

Let's start with moving to a new home, suburb or country. It certainly creates upheaval when we move. However, consider yourself staying in the same place all your life. This works for some people. They are the wise ones, who travel in their heads or in books. They can have many journeys and return home richer for their experience. I envy them. Having emigrated to Australia, I can say that while it was a huge upheaval. It transformed me, and I grew in ways I would have never grown had I stayed put. Yet, some of my siblings never moved; they had their own journeys.

My belief is that we all have a life path, and some of us miss it; we play it safe. That reliable job, that first relationship — it's all feeling like drudgery now. We acknowledge that we are unhappy, but we believe that this is our lot.

Most of us spend a lot of time at work. If we are appreciated for our contribution, treated with respect and are paid a salary commensurate with our position, that is great. However, if we are not, it is unhealthy for us to stay as it erodes our self-confidence, diminishes our performance and usually turns out bad for everyone concerned. Be mindful of your attitude towards your work. Only work in a company that has values you can align with.

We assume that our primary romantic relationship will last for a lifetime. In your heart, you know if the relationship you are in is for the long haul. Even if there are challenges, you will stick it out because it is worth it. However, if you are in a relationship where you feel stifled, unhappy, unappreciated or controlled, why are you staying? Is it because you think it is the right thing to do? Anything that is stifling your growth is not right for you. Any person who is not giving you breathing space to be yourself or supporting you in your journey of growth, is not worthy of your commitment. Always remember that a relationship is a two-way commitment, and if nothing is coming back your way, you are being short-changed. If you stay, **you are short-changing yourself**.

I am a big believer in commitment and longevity in relationships, but only when they are healthy relationships. So, ask yourself, should I stay or should I go?

Support
Lean in

As adults, we are all supporting something or someone — a cause, a charity, a person, a family, a friend.

Without us supporting our community, the world would be a much tougher place to live in.

Ask yourself how you feel about the support you give. Does it make you feel good? Or, do you feel burdened by it? It is important to think hard on this because if you are feeling burdened, you may need to consider this: Have you opened your heart to the importance of giving support? Perhaps you have, but you have overstretched in your capacity to do so. It is essential that everyone supports in some capacity. No matter how small our contribution is, it counts. So, don't overcommit; just do what you can.

> Everyone needs more support than they are getting.
> **Sheryl Sandberg**

What about the support you receive? Does it make you feel nurtured? Is it coming from the right place? Receiving is a gift we give to others. Humility helps us to understand why it is necessary to allow others to be our shoulder to cry on, or the hand we take when we are on a difficult path.

Self-support is also important! Ponder on this question: do you support yourself by understanding your needs and making sure they are met? Do you operate as an independent being that can stand on your own two feet? This does not mean that you won't need support every now and then. Knowing when you need support and when you can manage on your own is vital for your wellbeing. Supporting yourself, supporting others and receiving support is all part of living in a community. Embrace the joys of giving and receiving support.

Imagine

Imagination is the stepping stone of a new reality

If you can imagine it, you can manifest it. So, be careful of how you allow your mind to enter into this dream-like realm of imagination. Catch yourself if you are being negative and start again! You can use a little self-discipline; instruct your mind that only positive thoughts are welcome, and focus on a bright, clear future, without fear or negativity. Inevitably we'll all have ups and downs in reality, but if we can keep our thinking positive and stress-free, it will result in less anxiety. This can only be a good thing!

It is natural for us to want good things to happen and to feel good. So, use this wonderful tool, your imagination, to conjure up a vision of the life you would like to live and a state of being that will serve you well.

> Imagination is the highest kite one can fly.
> **Lauren Bacall**

When we think of all the great inventors — from way back when to modern times — the people who have the most impact are those who use their imaginations to create something no-one else has. They craft new ways of using old ideas and objects, and they invent completely new concepts that make our lives easier.

How does this apply to you? You have all you need to imagine a life for yourself that is better than the one you are living now. Do you have ideas about how you might make changes to make this new life a reality? Of course, you do. All it takes is imagination, courage and application! No matter how outlandish or unbelievable your imaginings are, they are there to inspire and motivate you., There's nothing holding you back. Start imagining it now!

Win/Lose

Sometimes we win and sometimes we lose

In this life, we often perceive people as either winners or losers. This is a judgement that we place on them. It can also be a judgement we put on ourselves and a damaging one at that. Yet, if we were to reflect on each cycle of our lives, sometimes we have won, and other times, we have lost. I don't believe there is a person on this earth that has not experienced both.

What we have to look out for is the mindset that we are a loser. It can alter the trajectory of our lives, when we come to believe that we cannot win. The middle ground is fine — understanding that there are "swings and roundabouts" in life, and we must navigate them all.

There is always a lesson that comes from losing. We incur simple losses, such as in a sporting event or a board game. Here, we are not talking about these simple losses; we are talking about losing a home, a job, a partner, a parent, a child, or even a pet. These are significant losses that come with emotional responses. They are also part and parcel of the cycle of life. No one escapes them. Understanding the grieving process can offer us some solace and help us to understand our responses are perfectly normal. According to Elisabeth Kübler-Ross, there are five stages of grief: denial, anger, bargaining, depression and acceptance[3]. We can move forward and backward through the phases during the period of our grief. So be kind to YOU and allow yourself to experience these feelings. Meditate on them and lovingly accept them as a natural response to the ebbs and flows of life.

There is always a lesson in winning too! Again, when we think of winners, we think of successful people: actors, sports champions and high-profile world figures. We hesitate to celebrate our own wins. That is, those meaningful wins. For example: when we conquer a health issue through persistence and perseverance; or when, against all the odds, we got accepted into the education program of our dreams. Just like we have observed with the grief cycle, we also have various emotional responses to winning. We can feel jubilation, elation or excitement. We can also feel guilty, unworthy or sad. Yes, sad! Of course, these negative feelings come out because on some level we don't feel worthy. There is so much complexity in our responses to winning that it makes Billie Jean King's quote — "A champion is afraid of losing. Everyone else is afraid of winning" — undeniable. We are often afraid of winning, afraid to be confronted with our own awesomeness.

When we react with guilt, sadness or feelings of unworthiness after a win, it is time to reflect on why these feelings dominate what should be a happy occasion. This may be the key to you understanding what is holding you back. Reflect on a time when you had a victory and perhaps were not as kind to yourself as you should be. Did you talk yourself down? Did you laugh it off and get embarrassed about it? Perhaps it is time to truly feel the joy of a win, sit with it and congratulate yourself. You deserve it.

Change

The beautiful butterfly is revealed through the process of change

Change is the only constant, they say. Yet as individuals, we can be quite resistant to change. We are in our comfort zones, in a fog of familiarity and habit; any suggestion of change can be seen as a threatening and disruptive event that we do not wish to endure. Some of us cope well with change and embrace it — welcome the unexpected visitor, change in weather. There are also those of us that respond very strongly to change that is unplanned. We fight it! We rail against it!

Have you have had the experience of moving house, city or country? All you can think about is the loss of the familiar, your friends, your neighbourhood and all the things that make you feel secure. Suddenly, you feel afraid of the unknown and angry that you are having this change thrust upon you.

Or, perhaps you have a secure job, in a company you have worked with for a while. Out of the blue there is a major restructure at work. You don't feel secure any more and your job is under threat. You didn't ask for this change, yet it is inevitable; it is going to happen anyway.

Even if neither of these scenarios applies to you, you will have been through something similar where you felt sudden change rear its head in your so-far predictable life.

But life is not predictable and change is relentless. Even when we seem to be in a stable and comfortable stage of our lives, change is like an undercurrent that is constantly stirring our spirits, urging us forward, towards our aspirations and dreams. Change may manifest as sudden uncomfortable events to shake us out of our complacency, but believe me, the undercurrent is always at work. Why? Because unless we are constantly in the driver's seat of our lives, moving towards our destiny, someone else has to take the wheel!

Reflect on your current situation and observe the subtle way in which change pervades your life. It can be internal, external, or both. Meditate on your forward movement. Rejoice that change is enabling you to release the stagnation in your life. When change is at play, you know you are alive. You may want to fight it, to resist it, but your energy is best spent embracing it because it is here, whether you like it or not.

Stillness

Be still and find your peace

In this busy life, it can be hard to sit still. It can be even more challenging to find a place where you can practice stillness. Yet, in this fast-paced life, stillness is exactly what we need.

It is tempting when we get home from a day at work, to rush to the gym, eat a meal, and tune in to Netflix. Or, maybe you prefer to stay head down, focusing on the social media channels on your devices? We seem to have lost the knack of resting and restoring our body, mind and spirit. We are in search of constant distraction until we fall into bed, exhausted, only to get up and do the same tomorrow.

Why stillness? There are many benefits to stillness. We need time to replenish our mental and physical energy, and time to unwind from the noise of the day. We need to get in touch with our inner selves, so that we can hear our inner wisdom. This is a time you can reflect on decisions you need to make and think about what positive changes you can implement into your life.

> Learning how to be still, to really be still and let life happen – that stillness becomes a radiance.
>
> **Morgan Freeman**

The first time I decided to be still, I felt very uncomfortable. I couldn't calm my busy mind and I thought of all the things I should or could be doing. However, perseverance pays off; I persisted. The outcome was surprising. I felt connected to my thoughts and more considered in my responses. I felt calmer and I wasn't rushing into decisions in a reactive way.

If you have never experienced meditation or mindfulness, it can be hard to know where to start. My suggestion is to keep it simple! If you have a quiet place where you can sit undisturbed, that is ideal. If you are sharing a home with others, perhaps use headphones to keep out any sounds that may distract you. One of the unexpected benefits of stillness is a sense of peace, contentment and connectedness. You will feel more confident using your intuition when making decisions, as you will be more in touch with yourself. One of the most valuable gifts you can give yourself is time alone in reflection.

When was the last time you were alone, in stillness and silence? Perhaps you can meditate on this, on the noise in your life and on how you might achieve inner peace.

Vulnerability
Open your heart

None of us like to feel vulnerable; we feel more open to pain, hurt and rejection. Yet, it's not that simple! While we are busy keeping all the negative feelings at bay, we build a wall to prevent ourselves from being vulnerable. The paradox is that this wall keeps the positive feelings out too. To fall in love, we must allow ourselves to be vulnerable. To be a great parent, we must also allow ourselves to be vulnerable. Everything that is worth experiencing requires us to be open.

Many people live half a life because of fear. They are afraid to commit, afraid to change, afraid to take a chance — they are afraid to be vulnerable! Don't be one of those people. When you meet someone new and you instantaneously like them, It is most likely because they are open to new experiences and meeting new people. They maintain a positive outlook, expecting most experiences to be good. Yes, some experiences will be less than good, bad even, but we must not shut the door on all experiences.

> Vulnerability sounds like truth and feels like courage. Truth and courage aren't always comfortable, but they're never weakness.
> **Brené Brown**

There is one reason we are on this earth and that is to live. To live, we must be open. Open to new opportunities, new experiences and new feelings. Being vulnerable is the perfect state to experience all that life has to offer. Sure, you will get hurt now and then, but you will also experience great joy and bliss. This does not mean you can't be discerning and look after yourself, but to close yourself off is to deny yourself valuable experiences that will make your life whole.

Acceptance
Go with the flow

At times, it is hard to accept outcomes, especially when we are vested in a particular result that does not eventuate. We don't always have control over the outcome. For instance, we may apply for a job we always wanted and get rejected. We could have feelings for someone and these feelings are not reciprocated. A friendship may end and we don't know why. These things happen all the time. Having control over an outcome is a misconception that gets shattered all the time! Suffice to say, we are more likely to accept how things will turn out if we have the self-respect to realise that it is okay to not be in control.

> I'm not wise, but the beginning of wisdom is there; it's like relaxing into – and an acceptance of – things.
> **Tina Turner**

If we want peace in our lives, acceptance is key. It is exhausting to fight for outcomes that you want in every situation. Of course this does not mean you can't have aspirations to achieve certain outcomes, and that you shouldn't work towards specific goals. The interesting thing then is that the journey is more rewarding than the destination. What is important is that we don't have a fixed mind-set about how things 'must' turn out, as invariably we will be disappointed.

We sometimes encounter people that we would classify as controlling. Yet, if we spend some time getting to know them, they often reveal that they are not so much controlling, as terrified of things being out of their control. It takes a lot of energy to try and control everything around you – it's exhausting! Also, it doesn't work. Simply said, some things are not ours to control, so unless you want a life of constant disappointment, sometimes it is good just to go with the flow.

Endings

Endings are mere punctuations in life

An ending can evoke a whole range of emotions, depending on whether it was initiated by you or it came upon you. If you decide to end something — a relationship, leave a job, walk away from a friendship — the first thing you might feel is relief. You might also feel guilt, fear or emptiness. When the ending is not of your making, the emotions may be the same but the intensity different.

There is this sense of security in things staying the same, and endings can make us feel "out of control" — in reality, we are! If someone else decides to end it with us, we are not in control of his or her decision. We can be angry, be distraught, feel empty or fearful, but at some point, we have to go on that journey towards acceptance.

It's not easy to accept an ending that someone else initiates! When this happens, the last thing we can believe is that there will be a good outcome. We need to experience the emptiness, the anger and the sadness before we can rationalise it and see that the cloud might have a silver lining.

One of the most distressing endings we may experience is the untimely death of a loved one. At times like this, it is hard to make sense of why. The feelings of grief, anger and loss are likely to be overwhelming for a time. The duration will vary depending on the circumstances.

It is hard to rationalise an ending such as this. If someone you care about is suffering, be there for them — listen to them, care for them, just BE with them. If you are suffering in this way, reach out to someone you can trust and let them be there for YOU. This is a time when all the support and love offered is most welcome, to help you through the difficulties you are facing.

When bad things happen, we need to allow ourselves to go through the whole range of emotions that descend upon us. Acknowledging these feelings is good. It is healthy to know why you feel the way you do. Allow yourself to step back with self-awareness; know that it is a journey and somewhere, further along the road, there is some relief. There will be another relationship, another job or friend.

Be kind to yourself in times like this. Allow your friends to commiserate with you; allow yourself to wallow. Don't forget to allow yourself to move on! Remember that endings can make way for wonderful new beginnings. Never give up your belief that the sun will shine again someday and that overall, life can be good.

Acknowledgements

I would like to thank my wonderful wife Karen for her unending support and encouragement throughout this process. Also, a huge thank you to my children and their partners who supported me and encouraged me along the way – Owen, Lib, Suzie, Paul, Christopher, Calisha. My two beautiful grandchildren who inspired my creativity and joy – Hugo and Aidan thank you! I am blessed to have so much support in my life.

My heartfelt gratitude to Aprill and Barbara, who were there for me right from the beginning, and who helped me 'workshop" my ideas – you helped make this project a reality.

Lori, who created beautiful illustrations, brought my words to life. Each picture tells a story, and I hope the readers are as inspired as I am by the wonderful images. In addition I will be eternally grateful to Tony, Lori's husband, who generously prepared the digital artwork to make it print ready.

Aly, my publisher, has been available along the way to give me the practical help and support I needed to get this project completed. Her belief in my book was a huge motivator to complete the journey.

The pre-purchase of my book has supported the publishing process, so thank you to all of my supporters listed below – you deserve full credit for getting me published! Many of you purchased multiple books – thank you all very much.

Aprill and Matt Allen
Mike Allen
John and Claire Barrett
Kerry and Joan Barrett
Tomas and Frances Barrett
Sr Mairead Barrett
Siobhan and Tom Barrett/Heffernan
Lauren Deahna, Jacob and Lucas Batson
Anne and Terry Biddulph
Wendy Bliss
Tristan Boot
Noelene and Stephen Bott
Sandra and Keith Buchanan
Lesley Case
Marilynn and John Cole
Karen and Alan Doodson
Rose Dyson
Paul and Cathi Edwards
Karen Ferris
Aisling and James Flood/Connolly
Anna and Vince Garuccio
Peter Grant
Anne Hamilton
Richard and Helen Harvey
Mary and Blair Healy
Kathryn Howard
Malini Jayaganesh
Breda and Joe Keane
Fiona and Micheal Kenny
Anna Kiss-Gyorgy
Sharon and Anthony Lawless

Veronica Leaney
Chris Lewis
Christopher and Calisha Lewis/Allsworth
Owen and Elizabeth Lewis/Schlyder
Debbie Louttit
Albert Matthews
Bernie and Vlado McMonagle/Ihasz
Jean McNamara
Anaïs Mendes
Berna and Bernard Mendes
Adelaide Mendes
Daragh and Brian Moloney
Jennifer Newport
Hugh and Cora O'Carroll
Patricia and John O'Sullivan
Victoria O'Reilly
Josh Pearson
Dean Penfold
David, Ria, Jed and Limor Reiss
Marie Scully
Giuseppe and Elaine Strati
Alex Strati
Bruno and Angela Strati
John and Rosa Strati/Mamakos
Julie, Dennis, Ben and Susie Talbot
Eschani Taylor
Suzie and Paul Thomas
Tania Thompson
Colette and Mick Thornton
Finola Walsh
Bridget Wardlaw

Help in times of need

Some conversations are just too complex for family and friends. Don't worry, you can either contact your trusted medical professional or one of these services:

Lifeline 131114

Suicide Call Back Service 1300 659 467

kidshelpline 1800 55 1800

GriefLine 1300 845 745

Endnotes

1 Cavalli, Thom F. Alchemical Psychology: Old Recipes for Living in a New World

2 Moore, Thomas. Dark Nights of the Soul

3 Kübler-Ross Elisabeth On Death and Dying

www.ingramcontent.com/pod-product-compliance
Lightning Source LLC
Chambersburg PA
CBHW041500010526
44107CB00044B/1516